LET'S FIND OUT! SPORTS

WHAT IS FOOTBALL?

SIYAVUSH SAIDIAN

Britannica Educational Publishing
IN ASSOCIATION WITH
ROSEN
EDUCATIONAL SERVICES

Published in 2019 by Britannica Educational Publishing (a trademark of Encyclopædia Britannica, Inc.) in association with The Rosen Publishing Group, Inc.
29 East 21st Street, New York, NY 10010

Distributed exclusively by Rosen Publishing.
To see additional Britannica Educational Publishing titles, go to rosenpublishing.com.

First Edition

Britannica Educational Publishing
J.E. Luebering: Executive Director, Core Editorial
Mary Rose McCudden: Editor, Britannica Student Encyclopedia

Rosen Publishing
Brian Garvey: Series Designer/Book Layout
Cindy Reiman: Photography Manager

Library of Congress Cataloging-in-Publication Data

Names: Saidian, Siyavush, author.
Title: What is football? / Siyavush Saidian.
Description: First Edition. | New York : Rosen Publishing 2019. | Series: Let's find out! Sports | "Distributed exclusively by Rosen Publishing—T.p. verso. |Includes webography. | Includes bibliographical references and index. | Audience: Grades 1-5
Identifiers: LCCN 2018026730| ISBN 9781538304754 (library bound) | ISBN 9781538304792 (paperback) | ISBN 9781538304884 (6 pack)
Subjects: LCSH: Football—Juvenile literature. | Football—United States—History—Juvenile literature.
Classification: LCC GV950.7 .S24 2019 | DDC 796.330973--dc23
LC record available at https://lccn.loc.gov/2018026730

Manufactured in the United States of America

Photo credits: Cover and interior pages background Eugene Onischenko/Shutterstock.com; pp. 4–5, 27, 28 Debby Wong/Shutterstock.com; p. 5 Scott Prokop/Shutterstock.com; p. 6 © Encyclopædia Britannica, Inc.; p. 7 Rey Del Rio/Getty Images; p. 8 Suzanne Tucker/Shutterstock.com; p. 9 Brocreative/Shutterstock.com; p. 10 Mark Herreid/Shutterstock.com; pp. 11, 12, 13 Aspen Photo/Shutterstock.com; p. 14 Richard Paul Kane/Shutterstock.com; p. 15 Dustin Bradford/Getty Images; p. 16 Bettmann/Getty Images; p. 17 John Panella/Shutterstock.com; p. 18 Icon Sportswire/Getty Images; p. 19 Hannah Foslien/Getty Images; p. 20 Library of Congress, Washington, D.C.; p. 21 Yale University/Getty Images; p. 22 Twin Design/Shutterstock.com; pp. 23, 25, 26 Focus On Sport/Getty Images; p. 24 Jason O. Watson/Getty Images; p. 29 Joseph Sohm/Shutterstock.com.

Contents

A New National Pastime

While baseball is traditionally regarded as America's national pastime, football has been the country's most popular sport for some time. Millions of people in the United States consider autumn to be football season. Football is a very popular sport that is played by people of all ages, from grade-schoolers to trained **professionals**. It involves running, passing, kicking, and body contact.

Vocabulary

Professionals are people who are paid to perform an activity.

The Saskatchewan Roughriders (with green helmets) and Edmonton Eskimos are two Canadian football teams.

A football game is played between two teams of eleven players each. A team scores points by moving a ball across the other team's goal line or kicking a ball through the other team's goalpost. The team that scores more points wins.

This game, sometimes called American football, is played mainly in the United States. Canadian football is similar to the US game. In most countries, the word "football" refers to the sport of soccer.

The New York Jets (in green jerseys) and Miami Dolphins are two professional football teams in the United States.

Playing Field and Equipment

Football is played on a grassy, rectangular field. The field is 120 yards (110 meters) long and 160 feet (49 m) wide. White lines called end lines and sidelines mark the edges of the field.

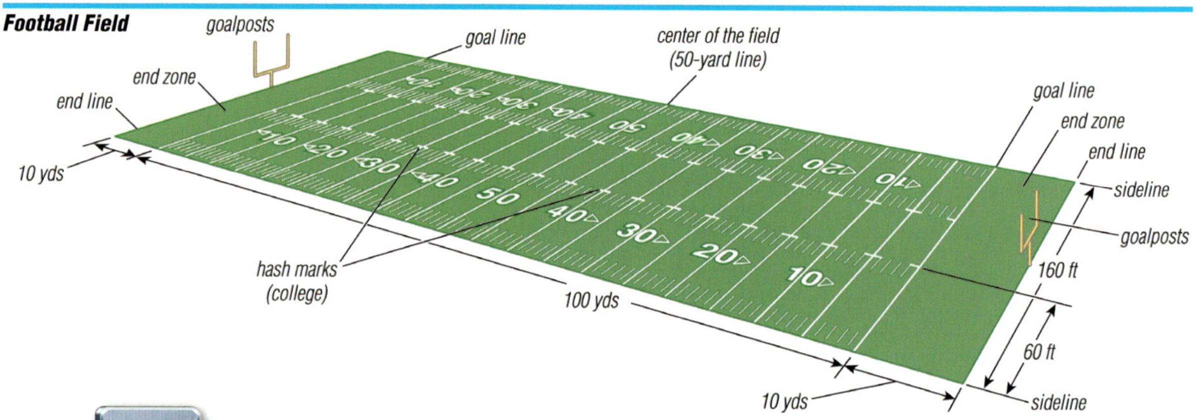

A football field has many markings that help officials, players, and viewers follow the game.

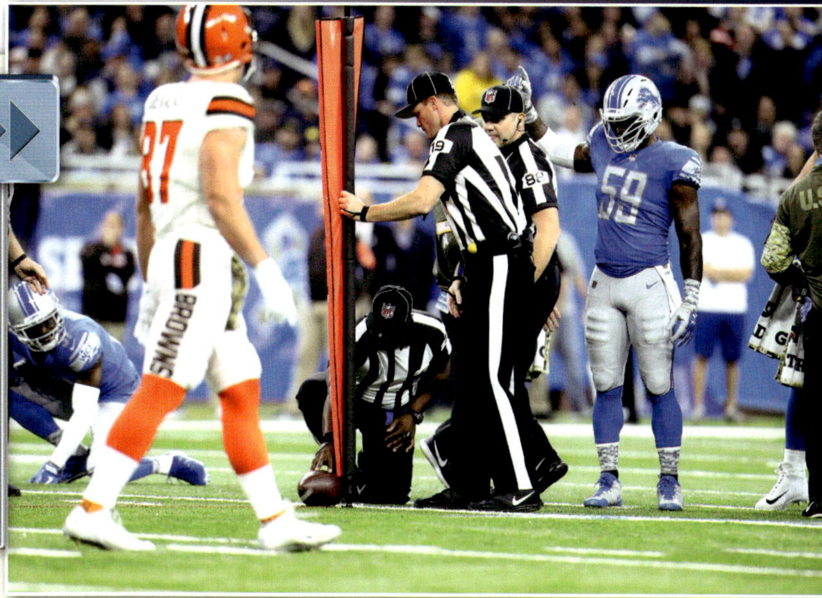

Officials, who wear black and white uniforms, sometimes use special equipment to measure how far a ball has been moved.

Each end of the field has a goal line. The goal lines are 100 yards (91 m) apart. The 10-yard (9.1 m) areas between the goal lines and the end lines are called the end zones. A pair of goalposts connected by a crossbar stands at the back of each end zone.

Most of the action in a football game takes place between the goal lines. White lines run across this part of the field every 5 yards (4.6 m). These lines help to show how far a team has moved the football. Two sets of short lines, called hash marks, cross these

Think About It

Why do you think a football field is so long?

lines. Officials use the hash marks to place the ball on the field after play is stopped.

Because football is a rough game, each player wears a plastic helmet with a face mask to protect his head. Players also wear pads to protect their shoulders, hips, thighs, knees, and forearms. Some players wear special pads and a thick jacket that cushions the ribs to help protect against specific injuries. Many players use a mouthguard. Players wear shoes with cleats, which dig into the ground and help prevent slipping.

All players wear helmets and shoulder pads to help protect their upper bodies from injury. A mouthguard protects a player's teeth, gums, and jaw.

Think About It

American football players wear a lot more padding than European football (or soccer) players. Why do you think that is?

The playing uniform consists of a jersey and tight-fitting pants that end just below the knee. The uniform has the player's number sewn on the front and back of the jersey.

A football is oval with pointed ends. It is filled with air and usually covered with leather. Even though most footballs are made with cowhide, they are sometimes called pigskins.

The shape of a football is unique. It is easier to throw and catch than a sphere-shaped ball, such as a basketball.

Playing the Game

A football game begins with a kickoff. One team, called the kicking team, kicks the football to the other team, called the receiving team. A player on the receiving team catches the ball. The player then runs toward the kicking team's goal line. The kicking team tries to stop them. Its players can

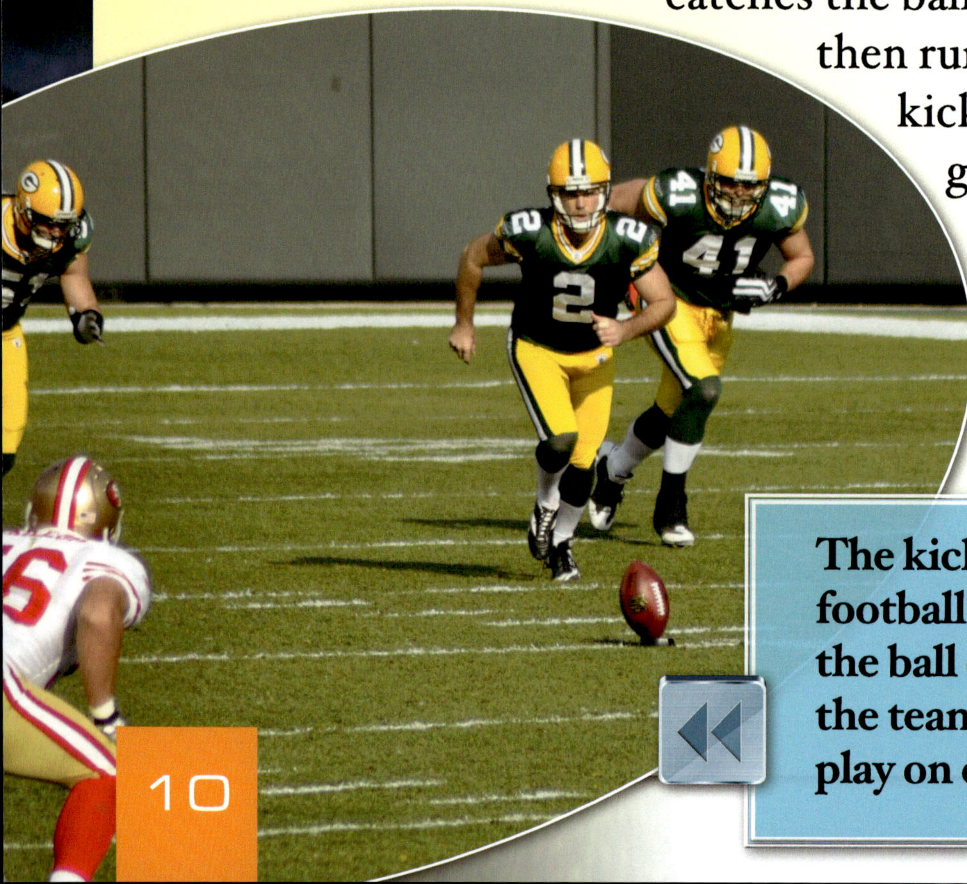

The kicker begins a football game by sending the ball down the field to the team that will begin play on offense.

tackle the ballcarrier or push him out of the playing area.

The game continues from the spot where the ballcarrier was stopped. An official places the ball on the field. The teams line up facing each other on opposite sides of the ball. An imaginary line runs sideline-to-sideline to separate both teams. This is called the line of scrimmage.

Vocabulary

A ballcarrier is any player who is holding the football and trying to move it toward the opponent's goal line.

Before each play begins, the offense and defense face each other over the empty space that is called the line of scrimmage.

The teams take turns playing offense and defense. The team with the ball plays offense. It tries to move the ball down the field to a score. The offense can move the ball by running with it or by throwing—or passing—it. The running or throwing tactics the offense uses are called plays. The offensive player called the quarterback begins most plays. The quarterback typically passes or hands the ball off to a teammate. The offense has four tries, called downs, to move the ball at least 10 yards (9.1 m). Each time they succeed, they get another four

A quarterback is typically the only player that passes the ball forward to a teammate. The quarterback also directs the offensive play of the team.

An interception occurs if a defensive player catches the ball, instead of an offensive player. The defensive team then becomes the offensive team.

downs to move the ball 10 yards. If the offense fails to move the ball 10 yards, the other team gets the ball.

The defense tries to prevent the other team from scoring. Defensive players may tackle ballcarriers. They can also catch a pass that the quarterback meant to throw to a teammate. This is called an interception. The team that catches the interception switches to offense.

Compare and Contrast

How are the roles of offense and defense alike? How are they different?

Scoring

The offense can score touchdowns or field goals. Running or passing the ball across the goal line scores a touchdown. A touchdown is worth six points. After a touchdown, the scoring team has a chance for more points. Kicking the ball between the goalposts is worth one extra point. Getting the ball into the end zone by running or passing earns two extra points. A field goal,

Offensive players are always trying to reach the end zone, which is often painted a different color so it is easy to see.

worth three points, is when the offense kicks the ball between the goalposts.

Compare and Contrast

What are some of the similarities of scoring on offense and defense? What are some of the differences?

Sometimes the defense scores, too. If an offensive player drops the ball, a defensive player can pick it up and carry it for a touchdown. A defensive player can also run with the ball after intercepting a pass. The defense scores two points if an offensive ballcarrier is tackled in their own end zone. This is called a safety.

If the defense forces a safety, the official makes this gesture. A safety is worth two points.

Pop Warner Leagues

Football is a sport that can be played starting from a young age. There are more than one million football players between ages six and twelve in the United States. For young players, the most popular organization is called Pop Warner. Named after the famous coach Glen "Pop" Warner, these leagues have special rules.

Glen "Pop" Warner became famous because of his success in coaching college football during the early 1900s.

Think About It

Why do you think some youth football leagues have age and weight rules? Do you think that is fair?

Unlike in high school, college, and professional football leagues, Pop Warner players must meet certain age and weight guidelines in order to play. To give everyone on the team a fair chance, each player must be allowed to participate in a minimum number of plays in each game. Certain types of blocking and tackling are also not allowed in Pop Warner leagues because player safety is a serious concern for young athletes.

Football can be played by people of all ages. Pop Warner and other youth football leagues are very popular in the United States.

SAFETY

Unlike many popular sports, football is usually full-contact. Players slam their bodies into one another and onto the field many times throughout the game. This can be dangerous, even when done properly. That is why players always wear pads and a helmet. Some people worry about the effect of all that contact. One version of the game—called flag football—does not allow tackling.

Every football league has rules in place to protect its players. Players and teams are penalized if they take certain actions.

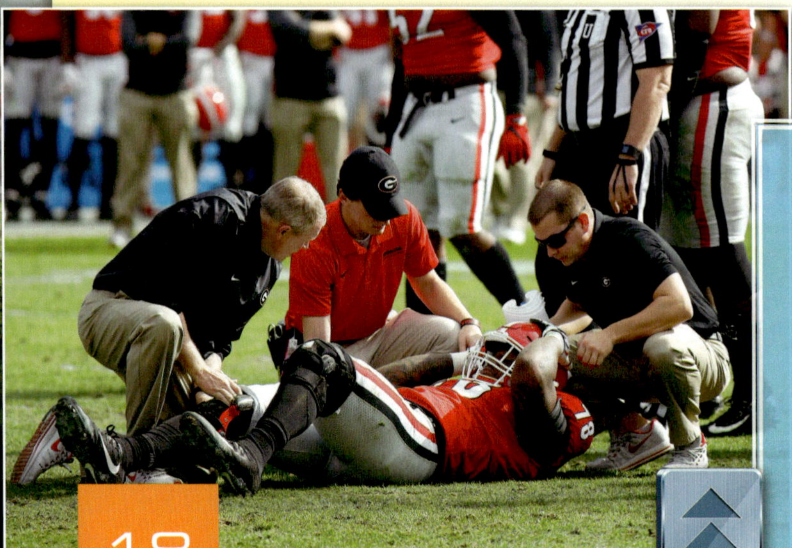

Even though there are rules and padding to protect players, injuries can sometimes happen, especially at the college and professional level.

A player who jumps to catch a ball is given special protection because he could get injured if he is hit the wrong way.

Some of the most serious penalties are for actions that could harm another player. These include chop blocks, or hitting an opponent's legs if they are already being blocked, and spearing, or butting with the helmet. Other fouls include pulling on a player's face mask and roughing the passer, or violently contacting a player after they have thrown the ball.

Think About It

What are some things football players are allowed to do that other athletes are not?

History

American football was first played in the late 1800s as a college sport. Princeton and Rutgers played the first college football game in 1869. This game was similar to soccer. In 1871, students at Harvard invented their own game. It combined parts of soccer with the English sport rugby. In 1876, representatives from several universities wrote a set of football rules.

Vocabulary

Rugby is an English game similar to football that is played without pads.

Dartmouth College was among the first to create and support a college football team, such as this one from 1901.

Walter Camp, a coach at Yale, helped separate the game of American football from rugby. Camp introduced the eleven-man team and the line of scrimmage. He also created the system of downs.

The first professional football game was played in 1895. In 1920, professional football teams formed the organization that would later become the National Football League (NFL). Since 1967, the two best teams in the NFL at the end of each season have competed in the Super Bowl.

Walter Camp and his Yale University football teams helped create the rules for the new sport.

THE NATIONAL FOOTBALL LEAGUE

The National Football League (NFL) is the major professional football league in the United States. Since 2002, there have been thirty-two teams in the NFL. The NFL is separated into two conferences: the American Football Conference and the National Football Conference. Each conference has four divisions (North, South, East, and West), with four teams in each division. Two big names in early

The National Football League's "shield" logo is familiar to many Americans.

Think About It

Why do you think the NFL separates its teams into conferences and divisions?

football were Earl "Curly" Lambeau of the Green Bay Packers and George Halas of the Chicago Bears. Lambeau's twenty-nine straight seasons as a head coach with Green Bay remained a professional record into the 2000s. Halas helped introduce improvements to football games, such as public announcement systems and radio broadcasts.

The NFL earns billions of dollars every year. It makes this money by selling broadcast rights to television companies, including ESPN, CBS, and Fox. It also sells merchandise, such as jerseys and hats.

George Halas was responsible for making modern football as popular and easy to watch as it is today.

THE SUPER BOWL

The Super Bowl is the yearly championship game of the NFL. The winner of the American Football Conference plays the winner of the National Football Conference. The game is in a different city each year.

The Super Bowl grew out of the merger of the NFL and American Football League (AFL). The first league championship game, called the AFL-NFL World Championship Game, was played in Los Angeles, California, in 1967. Since 1969, the game has been called

VOCABULARY

A merger is when two companies are combined.

The Green Bay Packers won the first football world championship before the game was called the Super Bowl.

the Super Bowl, with a Roman numeral counting each game—Super Bowl I, Super Bowl II, and so on.

The day of the Super Bowl, known as Super Bowl Sunday, has become an unofficial American holiday. The game is watched by more Americans than any other sporting event, and many Super Bowls are among the highest-rated television broadcasts in history.

Winning the Lombardi Trophy, shown here after Super Bowl LII, is the goal of every NFL team.

Famous Players

There have been many great professional football players. Jim Brown was a running back who played for the Cleveland Browns from 1957 to 1965. He led the league in rushing yardage every year except 1962. He was elected to the Pro Football Hall of Fame in 1971.

Lawrence Taylor, who played for the New York Giants from 1981 to 1993, is considered one of the best

Lawrence Taylor, shown here, is still respected as one of the best linebackers to ever play the game.

linebackers to ever play. He recorded more than 130 sacks and 1,000 tackles throughout his career. Taylor was elected to the Hall of Fame in 1999.

Vocabulary

Linebackers are defensive players who mostly play in the middle of the field to stop runs and short passes.

With 208 touchdowns, 1,549 catches, and 22,895 yards, Jerry Rice is considered the greatest wide receiver ever. Rice played for the San Francisco 49ers from 1985 to 2000. The team won three Super Bowl championships during that time. He joined the Hall of Fame in 2010. Many experts believe his records will never be broken.

Many football fans and experts believe Jerry Rice was the greatest receiver of all time.

Joe Montana was the quarterback for the 49ers for many of Rice's best years. He is also thought of as one of the best ever. He played for San Francisco from 1979 to 1992, during which time the team won four Super Bowls. During his career he threw for nearly 40,000 passing yards. He was elected to the Hall of Fame in 2000.

Until 2017, no quarterback had won more Super Bowl titles than Joe Montana, shown here.

One of the few quarterbacks who can compete with Montana's success is Tom Brady. He started playing for the New England Patriots in 2000. He has won more Super Bowl championships than any other quarterback in NFL history. He also led the team to a perfect sixteen-game **regular season** in 2007. Brady was named the NFL's most valuable player for a third time in 2017, when he became the oldest player ever (at age 40) to receive the honor.

Tom Brady, shown here behind his offensive line, has led his team to many Super Bowl appearances.

VOCABULARY

The regular season describes all the games played before the playoffs that lead to the Super Bowl.

Glossary

blocking The act of stopping or slowing the progress of an opponent in a game of football.

broadcast A single radio or television program.

championship A contest held to find a champion.

cleats A strip or projection fastened on or across something (as a shoe) to give strength or a place to hold or to prevent slipping.

conference An association of athletic teams.

elect To select by vote for an office, position, or membership.

goalpost One of two upright posts that serve as the goal in various games.

injury Hurt, damage, or loss received.

interception To take or seize on the way to or before arrival.

mouthguard A molded plastic guard inserted between a player's teeth.

oval Having the shape or outline of an egg.

penalized Given a penalty because of an illegal action.

sack The act of tackling an opposing quarterback behind the line of scrimmage.

slam To strike or beat hard.

spear To lead with the head or helmet when contacting an opposing player.

stadium A large usually roofless building with rows of seats for spectators at modern sports events.

tackle To seize or take hold of especially in order to stop or throw down.

touchdown The act of scoring six points in American football by carrying the ball over the opponent's goal line.

uniform Matching clothing worn by members of a particular group.

For More Information

Books

Bradley, Michael. *Pro Football's Underdogs: Players and Teams Who Shocked the Football World*. North Mankato, MN: Capstone, 2018.

Gramling, Gary, Beth Bugler, and Colin Hayes. *The Football Fanbook: Everything You Need to Know to Become a Gridiron Know-It-All*. New York, NY: Sports Illustrated, 2017.

Mikoley, Kate. *Football: Stats, Facts, and Figures*. New York, NY: Gareth Stevens, 2018.

Nagelhout, Ryan. *Football: Who Does What?* New York, NY: Gareth Stevens, 2018.

Rogers, Andy. *Who's Who of Pro Football: A Guide to the Game's Greatest Players*. North Mankato, MN: Capstone, 2016.

Websites

National Football League
www.nfl.com
Twitter, Facebook, Instagram: @NFL

Pop Warner Little Scholars
www.popwarner.com
Twitter: @Pop_Warner; Facebook, Instagram: @PopWarnerLittleScholars

Pro Football Hall of Fame
www.profootballhof.com
Twitter, Facebook, Instagram: @ProFootballHOF

Index